STORY OF BALANCE SHEET

Second Edition

Written By

J.P. Indora

Controller of Finance & Accounts

M.A. (English), B.Ed., PGDMM and LLB (Delhi University)

Disclaimer

It is purely a work of fiction to make understand the Accounting System. Any resemblance to any name or Person may be coincidence only, not for the purpose of causing hurt or harm to any person.

J.P. Indora

The Background

- Mohan Lal joined one of premier institute of Government situated at Delhi on 18.01.1997 as Section Officer (F&A) . For him, Balance Sheet was somewhat tough subject in the initial stage as he was not from the background of

- Commerce. Usually he used to visit one of the Big temple at Delhi where one of his best friend Mr. Sohan Lal was one of the Accounts Officers in the Satsang. He (Mohan) learnt the concepts of Balance Sheet from him (Sohan Lal) in June, 1998.

- W.e.f. 01.04.2003, New Accounting System on Accrual Basis was to be introduced in his department. Mohan Lal was somewhat confused regarding Accrual System. On 31st March, 2004, Mohan Lal visited the temple to meet his friend to take some knowledge on the closings of the Accounts so that proper Balance Sheet could be prepared for 2003-2004.

- He told him (Sohan) his (Mohan) problem about accrual accounting and about Balance Sheet of 2003-04 to be prepared after closing.
- Mohan:- Yaar, I am unable to understand this accounting system on Accrual basis.
- Sohan:- You show me your Balance Sheet of 2002-03.
- Mohan:- Ok, I show you.
- Sohan:- It is very simple.

Balance Sheet and its Parts

- Sohan:- Mohan, Do you know what is Balance Sheet and What are its Parts?
- Mohan:- No.
- Sohan:-Balance Sheet of any Institution is the Statement which contains the records of Assets and Liabilities of that particular Institute on a particular date. For example, In case that institute is to be closed permanently on a particular date , what will be its Liabilities to be cleared and what will be its Assets on that date. Apart from this Statement, there are two other Statements called 'Income and Expenditure Statement' and 'Receipt and Payment Statement'. All these Statements are prepared by the Institutions on the basis of Accounting Policies and Accounting Standards of the Government.

- Sohan (further tells):- 'Receipt and Payment Statement' is the Statement which depicts the Cash flow during the whole financial year. Money is received and Payments are made through out the year and all transactions of Receipt and Payments are recorded in this statement through various Registers. In 'Receipt and Payment Statement' all cash transactions are recorded whether these transactions pertain to Last Financial Years, Current Financial Year and Next Financial Year or pertains to Revenue or Capital.
- Mohan:- I got it. What is Income and Expenditure Statement?
- Sohan:- The Departments like yours which are not involved in trading and only gives services to the Society, but

to run the Institute, some earnings are required to make the expenditure for the institute. You must keep in mind that all receipts of money during the year are not Income of that particular year because the Receipts of money in the current financial year may also pertaining to Last FinancialYear or for Next Financial year. The receipts of money or payments pertaining to current financial year only, becomes the part of Income and Expenditure Statement of that financial year.

- Mohan:- Ohh! Now I came to understand why all money received in this year was not depicted in Income and Expenditure Statement.
- Sohan:- Mohan, Like all receipts, all payments are not part of Expenditure.

- The advance payments to employees or to private parties are not part of Expenditure, rather these are Current Assets of the Institute. Like wise, Advance Receipts of monies are also not the Income of that particular year in which the money was received. Although the money is received in current year but it pertained to either of the last year income or for the next year income. Receipt of the money or payments made in the current financial year are actually pertained to the financial year in which Services were given or received.
- Mohan:- Now, I have understood what the three statements are. Whether there are any rules or concepts to prepare all these three statements?
- Sohan:- Yes. Indian Government Accounting Standards (IGAS) have been issued by the DEA, Ministry of Finance to

form uniformity and comparability of Financial Statements of various organisations. The detailed about these Standards will be told to you some other day.

- Mohan:- Ok. I have heard about some Golden Rules of Accounting. What are these rules?
- Sohan:- 1st rule is 'Debit all expenses and losses', credit all incomes and gains'. 2nd is 'Debit the receiver, credit the Giver' and 3rd is 'Debit what comes in, credit what goes out'.
- Mohan:- Ok. What are Accounting Policies? I have seen these enclosed with the previous year Balance Sheet.
- Sohan:- To prepare Financial Statement, the Department implement specific procedures, Accounting Methods

and the procedure for presenting the disclosure etc.

- Mohan:- Ok. Are there some practical methods through which I can learn about 'Receipt and Payment Statement', 'Income and Expenditure Statement' and 'Balance Sheet' more effectively. In our village, people usually speaks as under:-
- (In vernacular)
- किसान लोग या व्यापारी लोग अक्सर यह बातें बोलते हुए सुने जा सकते हैं कि :-
- 1 व्यापार में लेन-देन चलता रहता है !
- 2 इस साल आमदनी से ज्यादा खर्चा हो गया क्योंकि इस साल फसल खराब हो गई , बारिश टाइम पर नहीं आई और जब आई तो ओले पड़ गए !

- 3 इस साल खर्चे से ज्यादा आमदनी हो गई क्योंकि इस साल फसल बहुत अच्छी हुई, बारिश बिल्कुल टाइम पर और सही हुई !

(In English)

- 1. "VYAPAAR ME LENA-DENA CHALTA RAHTA HA".
- 2. "ISS SAAL AAMDANI SE JYADA KHARCHA HO GAYA" KYONKI ISS SAAL FASAL KHARAB HO GAYI. BARISH TIME PE NAHI AYI OR JAB AYITO OLLE PAD GAYE.

- 3. "ISS SAAL KHARCHE SE JYADA AAMDANI HO GAYI KYONKI ISS SAAL FASAL BAHUT ACHHI HUI. BARISH BILKUL TIME PE OR SAHI HUI.

The above statements are in Vernacular)

- Mohan:- Whether the above statements are applicable in our 'Income and Expenditure Statement' or Balance Sheet or in any other statements?

- Sohan:- Yes, these sayings of village peoples are very much applicable in our 'Income and Expenditure Statement' and Balance Sheet.
- 1st saying **"VYAPAAR ME LENA-DENA CHALTA RAHTA HA" is applicable in Schedule-1, Sch-2, Sch-5, Sch-6 and Sch-8/Liability and Assets and are as per our Balance Sheet. We take advances/loans for Institute and also give loans/advances to employees and private parties as per Sch-1, Sch-2, Sch-3, Sch-4, Sch-5 and Sch-8 respectively.**

- 2nd saying "ISS SAAL AAMDANI SE JYADA KHARCHA HO GAYA" KYONKI ISS SAAL FASAL KHARAB HO GAYI. BARISH TIME PE NAHI AYI OR JAB AYI TO OLLE PAD GAYE", is related to 'EXCESS OF EXPENDITURE OVER INCOME' as per our I&E Statement).
- 3rd saying "ISS SAAL KHARCHE SE JYADA AAMDANI HUI" KYONKI ISS SAAL FASAL BAHUT ACHHI HUI. BARISH BILKUL TIME PE OR SAHI HUI, is related to EXCESS OF INCOME OVER EXPENDITURE' and is as per our I&E Statement.

- Mohan:-Ohh! It means villagers also know what is Income and Expenditure Account.
- Sohan:- Mohan, we have used much time to discuss about Balance Sheet, Income and Expenditure Statement and Receipt and Payment Account. Now, we must move further to see the R&P Activities practically and after that Income and Expenditure activities and lastly Balance Sheet.
- Mohan:- Ok.
- Sohan:- Mohan, We should go first to R&P activities as without Receipts of Money & after that Payments, Income and Expenditure can not be ascertained and after ascertaining Income and Expenditure on revenue account, we will move further to Current Assets and Advances and then to fixedAssets.

- And after knowing our Assets, we will move to Liability Section as all the Assets has been created through Liabilities only. No Liability, No Asset. If there are Assets, there is Liability also.
- (Now they move further to see actual activities. They see three Daanpatra in a Building and also see three water tanks fitted with In-let and Out-let pipes which are symbol of Receipt of Money in Daanpatras and Payments to various activities through various Buildings.).

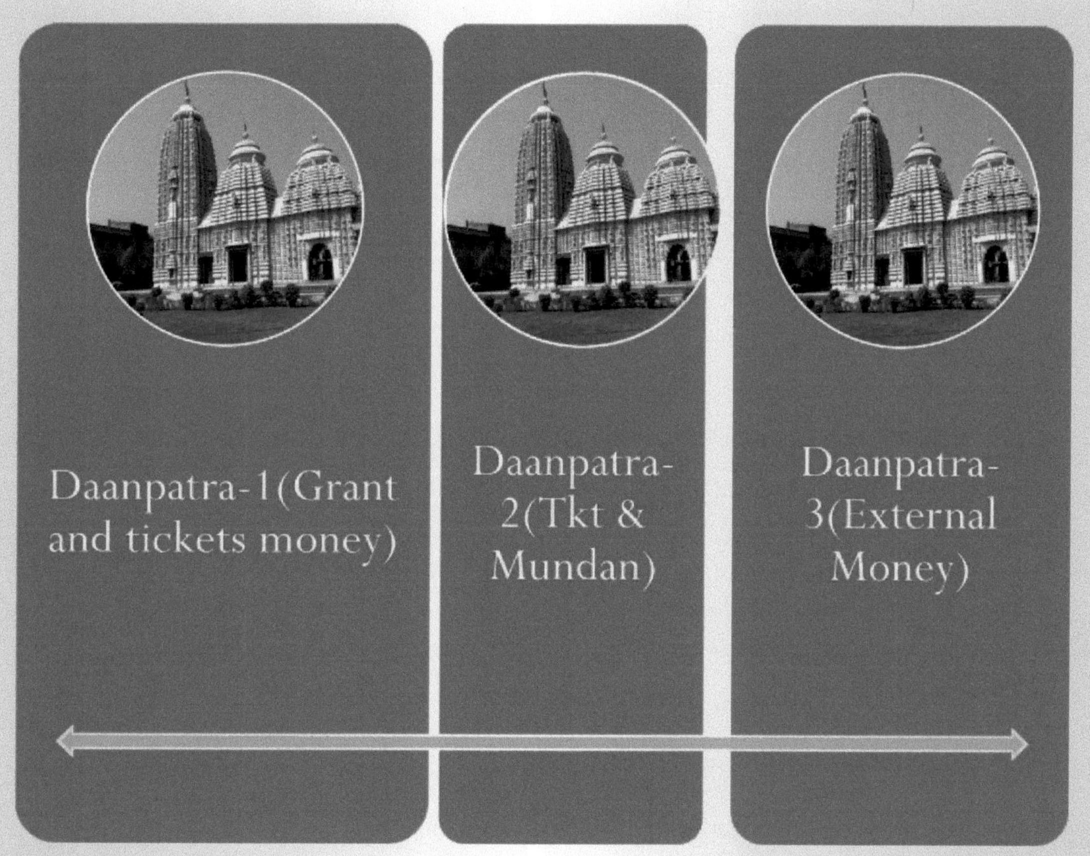
Daanpatra-1(Grant and tickets money)
Daanpatra-2(Tkt & Mundan)
Daanpatra-3(External Money)

PLUS
2 82 82 44
PLUS
2 82 82 44

- (Sohan takes him to the backside of the Temple and Show him three Daanpatra and from here Story of Balance Sheet starts).
- Sohan:- See this building and look at these three Daanpatras i.e. One very big and two smaller than this. These Daanpatra are like big water tanks from where water goes to various Buildings and various houses in the colony. These three Daanpatras are like Consolidated Fund of India, Contingency Fund of India and funds like PMCARES. This temple is controlled by the Government. One of the Government Department comes here every year after start of financial year and put crores of Rupees in the Big Daanpatra. Shardhalus

also come and give money in Big Daanpatra. 75% of Ashirwad money also goes to Big daanpatra. 25% of Ashirwad money goes to second daanpatra. The mundan ceremony is also performed in the temple and the fees taken for this purpose also goes in the second daanpatra and so on.

Being controlled by the Government, Our temple has good practice and we give receipt for the each penny we receive from the Government or Shardalus. Each and every transaction (Receipt/Payment) are recorded in the relevant registers without fail. Our Accounts are Audited by the State Government agency, every year.

(Near Daanpatras, some Parvachan is being given by some Baba ji)

- Mohan (Seeing the Baba ji):- I see he is Baba

Dharam Pal who is giving parvachan to Shardalus. There are queues of shardalus who are depositing the money. Do you people take money from shardhalus who come here to take Ashirwad from Baba Dharam Pal who is said to be privileged to receive Antargyan from some Goddess.

(They move further and go near Queues)

- Sohan:-Mohan, I have forgotten to tell you one thing.
- Mohan:-What is that?
- Sohan:- We have used Big ATM Machines through which the amount goes in Daanpatras, hence automatic calculation of money deposited in all the three Daanpatras. We also use Big ATM Machine at the main window of Daanpatras through which money is withdrawn and Small ATM Machines at the doors of Building No. 14, 13, 12, 8, 6 and 5 which automatic count the amount dispersed through each of them.

- Sohan(further tells):- On 31st March of each year we close all the windows of Daanpatra except window no. 8. The balance amount in each Daanpatra as on 31st March comes out through this window and automatic calculated and it is the Closing Balance on 31st March and It is depicted in Register No.8 as "Balance in Daanpatra". It is pertinent to mention here that the same amount will be again put in three Daanpatras as per their Balances and it will be treated as Opening Balance for the next financial year.

  (At this, Sohan Lal shows him his own Bank Statement and explains at next page)

Account Name : Mr. Sohan Lal
Address : Maharani Bagh, New Delhi
Balance on 1 Apr 2003 : 10,036.59
Start Date : 01-Apr-03
End Date : 20-May-03

Txn Date	Value Date	Description	Ref No./Cheque No.	Debit	Credit	Balance
02-Apr-03	02-Apr-03	TRANSFER CREDIT---	SWEEP FROM 41203972119		19,487.00	**29,523.59**
02-Apr-03	02-Apr-03	WITHDRAWAL TRANSFER---	TRANSFER TO 39032984421	29,000.00		523.59
02-Apr-03	02-Apr-03	TRANSFER CREDIT---	SWEEP FROM 41203972119		7,180.00	7,703.59
02-Apr-03	02-Apr-03	TO TRANSFER-UPI/DR/309303775923/J	TRANSFER TO 4693765162090	7,000.00		703.59
02-Apr-03	02-Apr-03	TO TRANSFER-UPI/DR/309311017335/N	TRANSFER TO 5097514162094	60		643.59
02-Apr-03	02-Apr-03	TRANSFER CREDIT---	SWEEP FROM 41203972119		2,052.00	2,695.59
10-May-03	10-May-03	DEBIT-ACHDr HDFC05813000028172 LIC	HousingFina--	24,709.00		952.71
10-May-03	10-May-03	TO TRANSFER-UPI/DR/313674057157/N	TRANSFER TO 4897691162095	199		753.71
10-May-03	10-May-03	TRANSFER CREDIT---	SWEEP FROM 41888292677		6,006.00	6,759.71
10-May-03	10-May-03	TO TRANSFER-UPI/DR/350326903279/R	TRANSFER TO 4897692162094	5,888.00		871.71
10-May-03	10-May-03	TO TRANSFER-UPI/DR/313770615577/S	TRANSFER TO 4897692162094	100		771.71
10-May-03	10-May-03	TRANSFER CREDIT---	SWEEP FROM 41888292677		2,002.00	2,773.71
10-May-03	10-May-03	TO TRANSFER-UPI/DR/350418899307/N	TRANSFER TO 4897693162093	2,339.00		434.71
10-May-03	10-May-03	TRANSFER CREDIT---	SWEEP FROM 41888292677		1,001.00	1,435.71
10-May-03	10-May-03	TO TRANSFER-UPI/DR/313968238195/B	TRANSFER TO 4897694162092	1,178.00		257.71
19-May-03	19-May-03	TRANSFER CREDIT---	SWEEP FROM 41888292677		1,001.00	1,258.71
19-May-03	19-May-03	TO TRANSFER-UPI/DR/313959218377/N	TRANSFER TO 4897694162092	445		813.71
19-May-03	19-May-03	TO TRANSFER-UPI/DR/313965455654/H	TRANSFER TO 4897694162092	110		703.71
19-May-03	19-May-03	TO TRANSFER-UPI/DR/313967547342/P	TRANSFER TO 4897694162092	450		**253.71**
			TOTAL	**2,56,273.88**	**2,46,491.00**	**-9,782.88**
				PAYMENTS	**RECEIPTS**	**DIFF.**

O.BALANCE	**10036.59**
RECEIPTS	246491
Tot OB+RECEIPTS	**256527.59**
PAYMENTS	256273.88
C.BALANCE	**253.71**

- Sohan (further tells):-All the three Daanpatras are like a Big Petrol Pump where Petrol, CNG and Diesal are dealt with. The Petrol, CNG and Diesal are stored in Big Tanks and through out the year all these three items are continuously supplied to the Tanks and from these tanks Petrol, CNG and Diesel are supplied to various vehicles like Bikes, Cars, Tractors, Trucks and many more vehicles through the Machines which calculate the supply of these three commodities. On 31st March of each year , the total supply in the Big Tanks and total consumption through out the year and Balance quantity is checked.

- In this way , total receipt ,total consumption and Balance is ascertained. It is like your Receipt & Payment account and it has no concern with Income and Expenditure. Whatever goes in and whatever comes out is "Receipt and Payment Account"
- (Now they move further to see the queues which were there and people were depositing the money).

Last Year Ashirwad taken Deposit Window (D)	Current year Ashirwad Deposit Window (R)	Next year Ashirwad Deposit Window (T)/Pre-paid receipt/Adv.receipt

- Sohan (Replies to Mohan):-Yes, the Shardalus buy tickets to attend Satsang. Tickets are also given on credit basis (Udhaar Basis) as our Shardalus are very honest person and also loyal to Baba ji. Baba ji has full faith in his Shardalus. Last year on 31.03.2003, Baba ji gave Ashirwad to Shardalus. Some shardalus could not pay on 31.03.2003 and after that Baba Ji was out of country and now he has come and they are paying now in this current financial year 2003-04.

In Ist Queue on 'D' Window, we are taking money for the Ashirwad provided on 31.03.2003 in the last financial year; In the second queue at window 'R' we are taking the money for this Ashirwad Satsang which is going on for the last 10 days; In the third queue at window 'T' we are taking advance payments for the Satsang to be held in next F. Year in June, 2004 for one month.(Lets move further where payments are being made)

Last Year Outstanding Expenditure Payment Window (S)	Current year Expenditure Window (P)	Pre-paid Expenses Window (E)

- Mohan (Further):- See, some people are taking the money from DaanPatra at window 'S' and some are at window 'P' and some are from window 'E' and getting it entered in the registers. Why is it so?
- Sohan:- At window 'S' the vendors are taking their payments which was not paid till 31.03.2003 although payable in f.y. 2002-03. At window 'P', the employees are taking money from Daanpatra to purchase AATA,

CHAWAL, DAAL etc. for Bhandara as well as for Stock purpose to be kept in central stores. They are also taking money for purchase of One Mercedes car for Baba ji and for some other equipments, computers, furniture etc.

- Mohan:- I think you make all expenditure (Revenue/Capital) from these three Dhanpatras?

- Sohan:- Yes. We make most of the expenditure from the Big Daanpatra and if sometimes there is lack of money in this Dhanpatra, we make expenditure from the Second Daanpatra. Third one is for outside parties only and expenditure is met from this Daanpatra for their own works only. Receipts in Daanpatras and Payments from them are like your 'Receipt and Payment Account'. All money comes in and goes out through these DaanPatras only.

- Mohan:- Ok, now I understood what is R&P Account. Please tell how you people record detailed transactions of Receipts and Payments.
- (Sohan takes Mohan further where there are Two Blocks i.e. Revenue Block (Block-A) from Building No. 14 to 9 and one unnumbered building for calculations of Income and Expenditure during and on the closing of the year; Capital / Asset Block (Block-B) from building no. 8 to 6;

Building no. 5 is Liability Calculation Building; The Reserve Block in Building no. 2; Capital Fund Building No. 1 and Balance of Liability & Asset Building without no.).

- Mohan:- Ok. Lets go there in each building one by one.
- Sohan (Taking him to each building one by one):- Look, this is Laboratory (Building No. 14) and lots of chemical, Consumables

and other related items are kept here to prepare sanitizer to kill insects. We purchase them from the market. Approximately Rs.4.00 Crore are used annually for this purpose. We use Register no. 14 to enter the expenditure transactions. This amount comes from Daanpatra-1 and sometimes from Daanpatra-2.

- Mohan:- Ok. It is like our Schedule 14.

- Sohan:-Yes.
- Sohan:- Please look at building no. 13. Electricity bills are being paid here and the building is also got repaired. We also make other Administrative Expenses on Electricity, Maintenance of Buildings, Colony maintenance, contingencies and on many other items to maintain the Temple properly. This expenditure is recorded in Register No. 13.

- Mohan:- I think it is like our Schedule 13. It is the expenditure like our P-04, P-06, P-701 and alike.
- Sohan:-Yes.
- (Sohan takes his friend Mohan further)
- Mohan:- Yaar, there is much crowd in Building no. 12. What this crowd is about?
- Sohan:- Some employees are being paid medical bill payments, TF, Bonus,

OTA, Hon., LTC payments etc. These payments are recorded in register no. 12. Through out the year except March salary, salary to all the employees has been paid through this window only.

- Mohan:- Ok, it is like our schedule 12 .
- Sohan:-Yes.

(They move further and they see some more queues of people in another section i.e. Receipt section).

Income Window 11('R') Employees	Income Window 11 ('R') Employees & Others

- Mohan:- Please see building no. 11 where people are standing in the rows. What are these rows?
- Sohan:-Some empty drums are being sold there and people are depositing the purchase money. In second line people are depositing Licence Fees for their quarters and for some other misc. works. These receipts are recorded in Register no. 11.
- Mohan:- Ohh! It is like our schedule 11. (They move further and they further see two Queues)

Income Window 10('R') Bank Officials	Income Window 10 ('R') Employees

- Mohan:-Why there is crowd in building no. 10?
- Sohan:- In first line, these are officers from the Banks who are depositing the Interest Amount on term deposits, on saving account and interest on margin money etc due upto February 2004. The next interest will be deposited by them on 30.04.2004. In the second line, employees are depositing interest on loans like HBA, PC and Conveyance etc. due upto 31.03.2004 i.e. in this

financial year only. These receipts are recorded in Register no. 10.

- Mohan:- It is like our Schedule 10.
- Mohan:- For what purpose this Building No. 9 is?
- Sohan:- Our Accounts Officer dealing with revenue expenditure sits in this building and now he is calculating how much money has been utilized on Revenue

Account from Government grand(Daanpatra-1) and from Reserves (Daanpatra-2). It is pertinent to mention here that Daanpatras are kept in a Building in between building no.14 & 8 before Block-A and Block-B starts. In Block-A, from Building No. 14 to building No.9, the Register no. 14 to 12 for Revenue Expenditure and Register No. 11 to 9 for Revenue Receipts, are maintained properly.

- The register No. 9 is meant for the records how much money has been utilized from the money given by the Government in big Daanpatra-1 and how much money has been utilized from the Second Daanpatra-2 etc.

- Mohan:- Ohh! It is like our schedule 9 and the first Daanpatra is like money in the form of Govt. GRANTS and Second Daanpatra is like Reserve Fund.

- Sohan:-Now next building is there where another Accounts Officer sits to calculate the total expenditure from the Register No. 14 to 12 and total revenue receipts from the register no. 11 to 9. The figures of Increase/Decrease of Inventories are also recorded here being income. The figures of Depreciation as per Register 6 are also recorded being loss. We call this Register "Income and Expenditure Statement".

- The Accounts Officer fills the figures of income and expenditure from register no. 11 to 9 and 14 to 12 respectively in the Register of Income and Expenditure. Loss on account of Depreciation is also accounted for in this register as Expenditure, the entry taken from Register no. 6. Increase/Decrease of Inventories is also accounted for in this register as Income, the entry taken from Register no. 8.

- The total figure of expenditure is subtracted from the total figure of Income. If the figure of Income is more than the Expenditure, the figure is shown under "Balance being excess of Income over Expenditure" and If the figure of Income is less than the Expenditure, the figure is shown under "Balance being excess of expenditure over Income" and figure also goes in Capital Fund Register No. 1.

- Mohan:- It is also like our Income and Expenditure Account.
- Sohan:-Yes.
- Mohan:- I think this Block-A of Revenue Expenditure & Revenue Receipt after Income and Expenditure Statement building comes to end here. Where to go now?

Accrued Income ('I') Window	Outstanding Expenditure Window ('O')

- Sohan (Giving Sign to two Queues):- Please see the Queues at the start of Capital Block. These are very important windows for Accrual system. Now we will go to Capital Block which is in another line of buildings i.e Block-B.
- Mohan:- Ok.

- Sohan:- See this is building no.8 and all records are maintained in register no. 8. All the transactions relating to Current Assets including Stock Inventories purchased from revenue heads and are lying in stock of Central Stores which is adjacent to this building no. 8; Cash & Bank Balance; Advances to employees (Both interest bearing and non-interest bearing); pre-paid advances; Accrued Income;

advances and other recoverable payments; excess expenditure on external projects; advances for ECF; Recoupment due-PF and others etc; are recorded in Register no. 8.

- Mohan:- It is like our schedule no. 8.
- Sohan:-Yes.
- Mohan:- What is this building no. 6? It is very big building.
- Sohan:- Our fixed Assets purchased out of capital

grant like Apparatus & Equipments, Workshop Machinery, Computer Equipment/Major Computer software, Office equipments, furniture & fittings, Model & Exhibits, Vehicle and Transport, Tools & Plants, Electrical installations and equipment, Library books etc. are placed in this building and the transactions are recorded in Register no. 6. The other transactions like

- Work-in-progress and electronic journals are also recorded in this register.
- Mohan:-Sohan, the date of purchase and amount of purchase has been mentioned on all the items placed in building no. 6 and on most of the items year wise amount of depreciation and net value in reducing way has been mentioned. Some new Cars are also standing in the building but no amount of

depreciation has been mentioned on them. Why all these amounts are mentioned on the items?

- Sohan:- Mohan come here and sit in the car. I will show you something. See, all the copies of year wise insurances of the car. In the year of purchase of car, the value of car has been shown as full value of Car. In the next year, value of car has been somewhat reduced. In the second year, the value is further reduced and so on. It is the 15th year of this car and the value has been mention as Rs. ONE only. The life span of car has been fixed by the Government at 15 years only.

- The value of this car has been continuously reduced in the insurance policy. Reduction of the value of car year to year is Depreciation charged. Now this car has been sold in Auction to a

Kabari for Rs. 25001/-. In this way , the profit of Rs. 25000/- has been occurred and this profit of Rs. 25000/- will be accounted for in Register no.11 under the head "Profit on sale of Assets". The asset will be written off from the register no. 6 through C-Voucher and the residuary value of car i.e. value of Rs.1. It will be recorded in Register no. 13 under the head "Assets written off".

- Like this transaction, other items are also depreciated keeping in view their life span and loss on account of written off of Asset is accounted for in register no. 13 and sale value of written off Assets will be accounted for in Register no.11 under the head "Profit on sale of Assets". The land and Buildings on which this temple is situated are also accounted for in register no. 6.

- Mohan:- Now, I understood what is our schedule-6 (Fixed Assets). Now I understood why different percentage of depreciation has been fixed for different items in schedule-6. Each type of item has its own life span and accordingly the percentage of depreciation has been fixed.
- Mohan : - What is capital expenditure ?
- Sohan : - By incurring capital expenditures, we either increase over assets, or reduce the Liability. For example, if we repay our loans etc., the liability is reduced.
- Mohan:- Who are there in building no. 5 ?

- Sohan:- Lets visit building no. 5 and you will yourself know who they are.
- Sohan:- They are the persons who had given the amount in Big Daanpatra, Second Daanpatra and 3rd Daanpatra. They are here to know the status of their money i.e. How much is balance. They are Lendaar (Creditors). In addition to them, there are officials from other departments like Income

- Tax etc. to take I.tax yet to be paid by the temple.
- Mohan:- There are none in building no. 4 and 3. These are empty. What about next?
- Sohan:- Now we will visit building no. 2 where Accounts Officer is checking the transactions of money in Register no. 2. He is checking how much amount was generated during the year in this second Daanpatra and how much was utilized on Capital account and Revenue

Account. He is checking how much is balance in the Second Daanpatra and Register no. 2. After ascertaining the correctness of the amount he will move the balance in Balance Sheet.

- Mohan:- Ok, now I understood about register no. 2. It is like our schedule 2 (Reserve Fund). What next?
- Sohan:-Next is Building no. 1. All the transactions are recorded in Register no. 1. It is called Capital

Fund. All the transactions related to capital expenditure are recorded in this register no. 1. Even balance in the form of Cash or Kind from Income and Expenditure Account is recorded here. The total of Capital Fund is carried to Balance Sheet of the year under Liabilities Head.

- Mohan:- Ok, now I understand. What is next?

- Sohan:- Now it is the register of Balance Sheet called Balance Sheet itself. The totals of Register No. 1, 2 and 5 are recorded under the head "Liabilities" under different headings and the totals of Register No. 6, 7 & 8 are recorded under the different heads of Asset side of Balance Sheet. If Difference of Asset and Liabilities is "NIL", then Balance Sheet is OK.

- (Now, Mohan was having the perfect knowledge of what was Balance Sheet and Mohan continued to prepare the proper Balance Sheet.
- There is Accrued Income and also Outstanding Expenses for the F.Y. 2003-04 which are being entered in the proper registers (As per the Queue in next page) which will be received/paid during 2004-05.

Accrued Income ('I') Window	Outstanding Expenditure Window ('O')

- Sohan:- In first line, these are officers from the Banks who are giving the figures of the Interest Amount on term deposits, on saving account and interest on margin money etc due as on 31.03.2004, not actual payment. In the second line, the employees are standing only to get their salary slip to know the amount of their salary which is although due on 31.03.2004 but it will be disbursed on 01.04.2004 or on later date.

- (Now Sohan is clarifying many salient features to Mohan through the actual activities. The pictures of activities which are being done on dated 31.03.2004 are again shown to Mohan)
- 1. Shardalus and others are depositing the money in Daanpatras and getting the money receipts which will be accounted for in different registers as mentioned in the Story. Unauthorized deposit in Daanpatra is not allowed. Bank

account of the temple is not disclosed to anyone like departmental account of some of the Departments who only authorise some of the branches of Banks to take cheques/DDs on their behalf.

- 2. Money is being dispensed off from Daanpatra-1 and sometimes from Daanpatra-2 through the taps, for the expenditure (Revenue & Capital) by the officials in Building No. 14,13,12,8,7,6 etc. to pay to the employees as well as to the private parties.

- 3. In First Block, presently there are seven Buildings (Left to Right) i.e. Building No. 14,13,12,11,10,9 and one last building without number.
- 4. In the second Block also, presently there are seven buildings (Left to Right) i.e. Building No.

- 8,7,6,5,2,1 and One without number. In Building no. 5, the transactions (Receipts & Expenditure) of Daanpatra-3 are accounted far.
- 5. It is informed that Building in which Income and Expenditure Statement is being prepared, is without number as there are no receipts or expenditure from this building and is last in the Block.

- 6. It is informed that Building in which Balance Statement is being prepared, is without number as there are no receipts or Payments from this building and is also last in the Block.

- **Government Official are standing in Queue to give Daan in Daanpatra-1**

Last Year Ashirwad taken Deposit Window (D)	Current year Ashirwad Deposit Window (R)	Next year Ashirwad Deposit Window (T)/Pre-paid receipt/Adv.receipt

Daanpatra-1(Grant and tickets money)
Daanpatra-2(Tkt & Mundan)
Daanpatra-3(External Money)

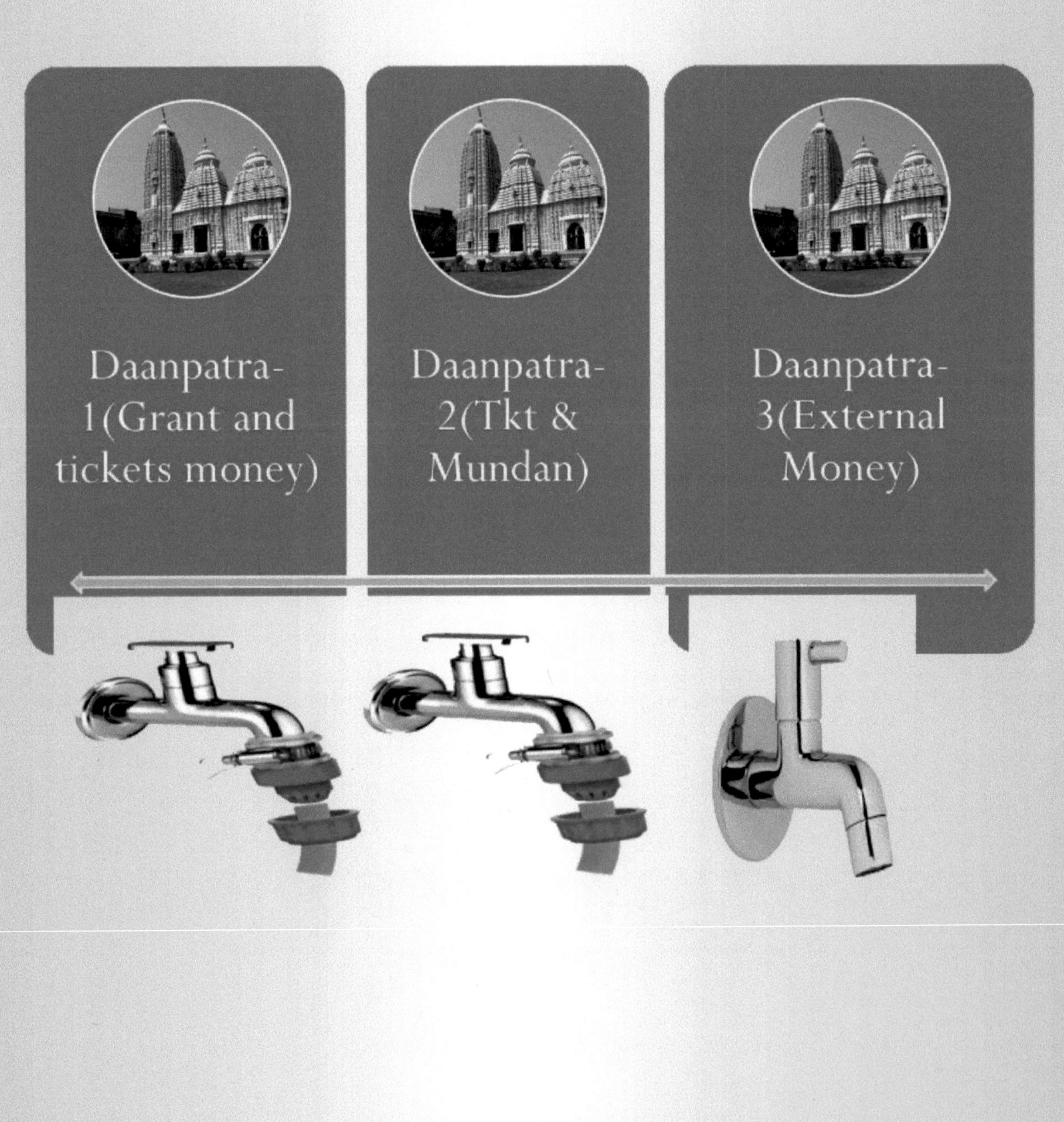
Daanpatra-1(Grant and tickets money)
Daanpatra-2(Tkt & Mundan)
Daanpatra-3(External Money)

Story of Balance Sheet

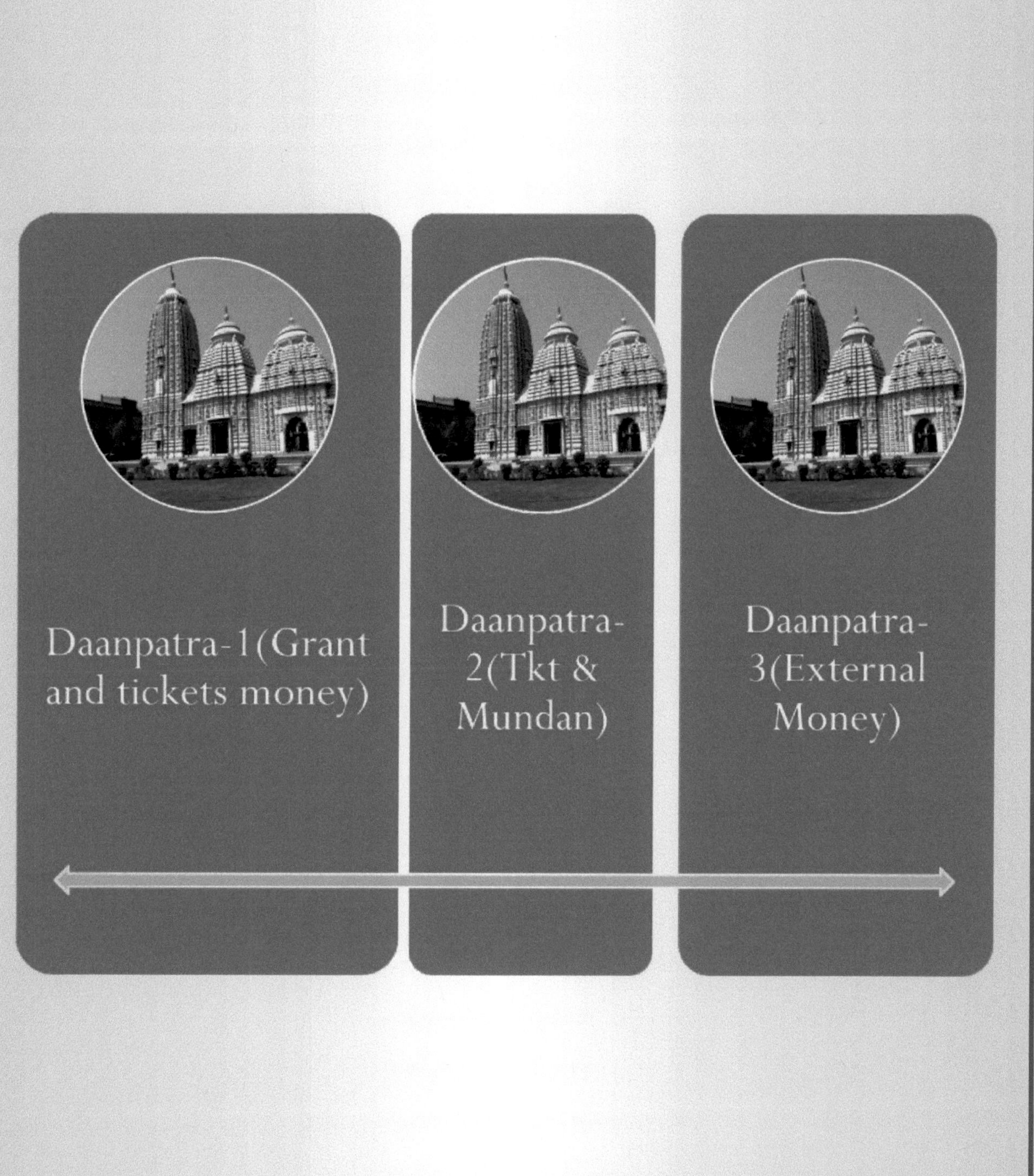

- Block-A (Revenue Block):- Building No.14,13,12,11,10,9 and N.
- Block-B (Capital Block):- Building No. 8,7,6,5,2,1 and N.

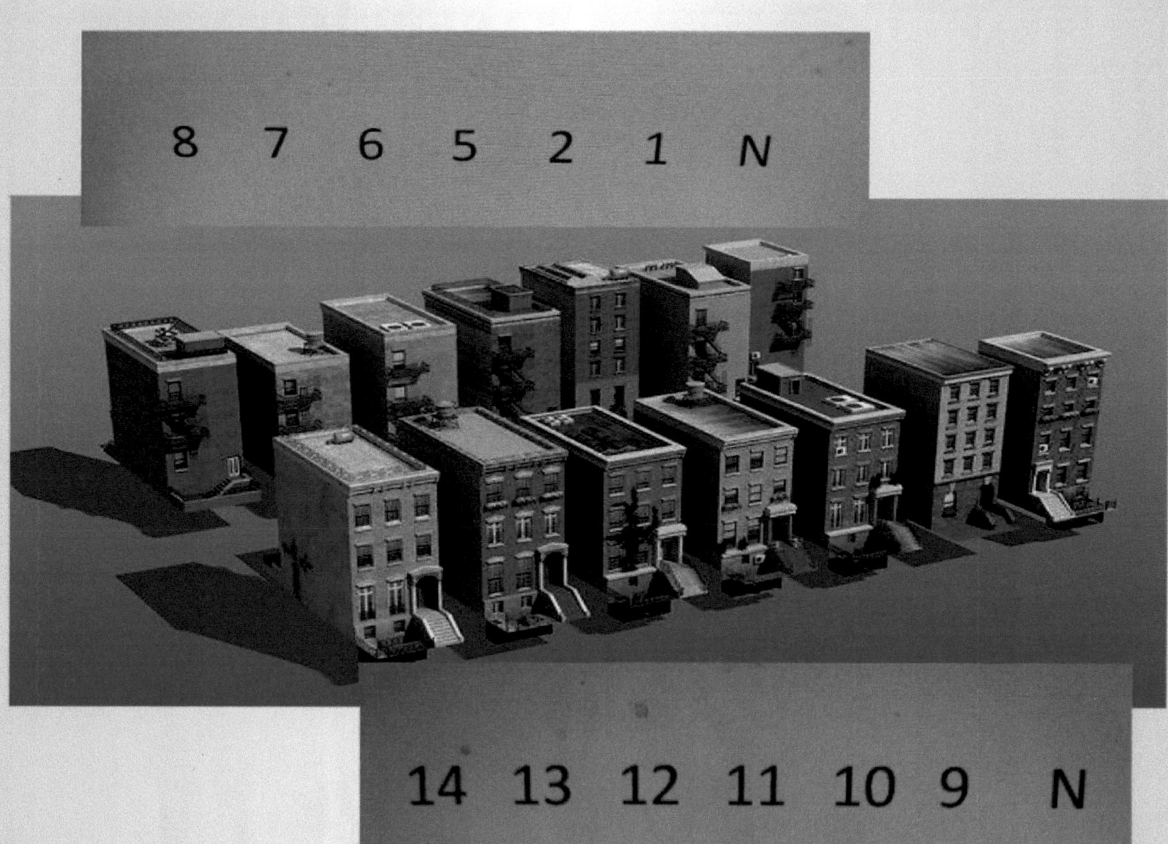
8 7 6 5 2 1 N
14 13 12 11 10 9 N

Accrued Income ('I') Window	Outstanding Expenditure Window ('O')

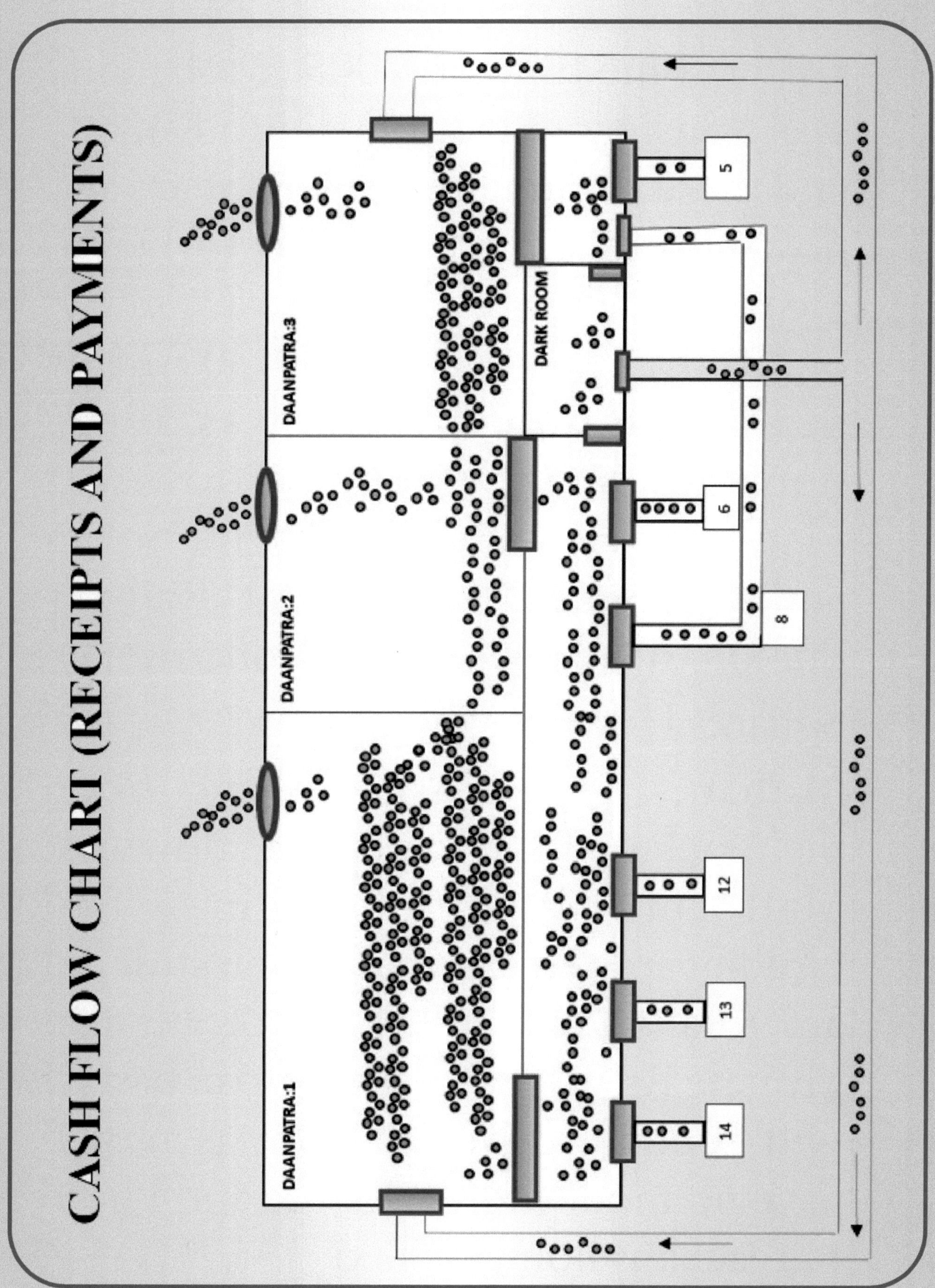
CASH FLOW CHART (RECEIPTS AND PAYMENTS)
DAANPATRA:1
DAANPATRA:2
DAANPATRA:3
DARK ROOM
5
6
8
12
13
14

- (After some time, in 2009 Mohan Lal was transferred from Delhi to Kolkata and there he remained for 14 years and now he is again transferred to Delhi. He reaches New Delhi Railway Station on 30.05.2023 at about 10.30 AM by Sealdah Rajdhani. He was pick-pocketed as he stepped down at Platform. He called his friend Sohan and he (Sohan) reached at Railway Station to meet his friend Mohan).
- Sohan:- How are you, Mohan?
- Mohan:- Don't ask! I have been pickpocketed as I stepped down at platform. My Mobile, Purse and Credit cards etc., all have been stolen. I am totally confused. First of all, you give me Rs. 1000/- cash on loan basis. I will return you tomorrow as now I have no money left with me and I have to reach my home by Taxi.

- Sohan:- Ohh! So sad! (Sohan gives him one thousand rupees in Cash).
- Mohan:- Sohan, Give me your Paytm number.
- Sohan:- Ok. I give you my Paytm number.
- Mohan (on 31.05.2023 telephonically):- Mohan, I have paid you Rs. 1000/- through my Paytm and I have received a message from my bank that my account has been debited for Rs. 1000/- (Rs. One thousand only). I have also taken Bank Statements of yours and mine from the Bank as I had gone to Bank to meet my friend Rahul who is Bank Manager there.
- Sohan:- Ok. I have also just received the message on my mobile regarding credit of Rs. 1000/- (One thousand) in my saving account.

- Mohan:- (Mohan meets Sohan in the evening on 31.05.2023). Sohan, these are our Bank Statements of today dated 31.05.2023. Please check them and tell what these statements teach us.
- Sohan:- Ok, I tell you. Please see both the Bank Statements and see the transactions of Rs. 1000/- (One thousand). In my statement, I paid Rs. 1000/- to you and amount has been shown as "Debit" and as per the descriptions, you were the receiver of money; In your statement, the amount of Rs. 1000/- given by me has been shown as " Credit" as I was giver of money. It is the case of dated 30.05.2023. Now, see the transactions of today i.e. 31.05.2023.The reverse is the case.Today you paid Rs. 1000/- to me and amount has been shown as "Debit" in your statement and as per

the descriptions, I was the receiver of money; In my statement, the amount of Rs. 1000/- given by you has been shown as " Credit" as you were the giver of money. The fundamental principle of accounting i.e. "Debit the receiver, Credit the giver" has been fulfilled. Debit is shown with "TO", Credit with "BY".

- Mohan:- Ohh! How you have applied the principle in Bank Statement!
- Sohan:- Mohan, even Rs. 1000/- was Liability for you until you repaid it and it was Current Asset for me until I received my money back. Now, you have no Liability of Rs. 1000/- on your head pertaining to me and I have no current Asset i.e. Accounts receivables of Rs. 1000/- from you.

- Sohan (Further):- When you were keeping my money of Rs. 1000/- with you, the Liability and Asset were equal. Rs. 1000/- was in your custody, so it was Asset for you and you could have spent it for any purposes; on the other hand, Rs. 1000/- was Liability for you as it was to be repaid to me by you.

Account Name : Mr. Sohan Lal
Address : Dwarka, New Delhi

Date : 31-May-23
Account Number : _0000007379
Account Description: SBCHQ-CSA-PUBIND-CSSILVER-INR
Branch :
Drawing Power : 0
Interest Rate(% p.a.): 2.7
MOD Balance :
CIF No. : _85557861522
IFS (Indian Financial System) MBIN0006948
MICR (Magnetic Ink Charact _826002014
Nomination Registered : Yes
Balance on 30 May 2023 243.4
Start Date : 30-May-23
End Date : 31-May-23

Txn Date	Value Date	Description	Debit	Credit	Balance
30-May-23	30-May-23	TRANSFER CREDIT---		1,006.00	1,249.40
30-May-23	30-May-23	TO TRANSFER-UPI/DR/3516	1,000.00		249.4
31-May-23	31-May-23	BY TRANSFER-UPI/CR/3517(		1,000.00	1,249.40

**This is a computer generated statement and does not require a signature

Account Name : Mr. Mohan Lal
Address : Maharani Bag, New Delhi

Date : 31-May-23
Account Number : _00000039106547626
Account Description: REGULAR SB CHQ-INDIVIDUALS
Branch :
Drawing Power : 0
Interest Rate(% p.a.): 2.7
MOD Balance : 0
CIF No. :
IFS (Indian Financial System MBIN0001670
MICR (Magnetic Ink Charact _826002007
Nomination Registered : No
Balance on 30 May 2023 1,168.50
Start Date : 30-May-23
End Date : 31-May-23

Txn Date	Value Date	Description	Debit	Credit	Balance
30-May-23	30-May-23	BY TRANSFER-UPI/CR/35161		1,000.00	2,168.50
31-May-23	31-May-23	TO TRANSFER-UPI/DR/3517(	1,000.00		1,168.50

**This is a computer generated statement and does not require a signature

- (Now both friends go to temple to eat food from Bhandara)
- Mohan:- Sohan, here are baskets full of breads (Chapati) and Rice and Utensils full of cooked Pulses (Daal)!
- Sohan:- Mohan, take breads (Chapati) and count them how many breads you can eat, nowadays.
- Mohan:- Ok.

  (They both take plates, spoons and glasses for water and sit on the floor to wait for food to be served)
- Serviceman (Sevadaar in Bhandara at Temple):- Chapati! Chapati!

- Mohan:- Give me two Breads (chapaties) only in the first instance and place them in my plate.
- Serviceman:- Ok.
- Sohan:- Mohan, today you have eaten 10 breads (Chapaties) and your plate was always full of cooked pulse (Daal). I think you are fond of Daal.
- Mohan:- I fully enjoyed the food in Bhandara (in temple).

- Sohan:- Mohan, I saw your plate received 10 breads from serviceman's basket. At one time, it became empty. The breads were coming in your plate and going out of basket. The principle of "Debit what comes in, Credit what goes out" was applicable in your eating.

  (Both friends come out and go to market near temple)

- Mohan:- Sohan, I want to take some cold-drink. (He buys two bottles of cold-drink for the both and pay Rs. 70/- to the shopkeeper through Paytm. He receives the message of Debit his account by Rs. 70/- on his mobile phone. He shows the message to Sohan and Sohan explains him how the transactions are recorded in Bank Statement of Mohan and Shopkeeper).

- Sohan:- Mohan, you have paid Rs. 70/- to the Shopkeeper. Here the Shopkeeper is the receiver of money. Rs. 70/- is expenditure for you and Income for the Shopkeeper. In your bank statement this amount will be shown as "Debit" and in the statement of Shopkeeper it will be shown on the side of "Credit". The principle of "Debit the expenditure or loss and Credit the income or gains" is applicable in this transaction of Rs. 70/- paid by you for the two bottles of cold-drinks. Rest of the things I will tell you at any later date as it is too late to go to home. We will meet soon again.

(Both friends say bye-bye to each other and go to their own homes. Mohan learns the transactions of Debit and Credit).

AUTHOR'S COMMENTS

- Whenever any person (Individual, Shareholders or the Government Institute) wishes to establish any Business or to create any Institution for the Societal Purposes, they have to invest Capital before starting the Business. They have to purchase Land, construct Buildings, Purchase of Furniture and other Capital Items like Computers etc. based on the requirements of the Business. Some amount of money in the form of Cash is also invested in the Business to run the business or Institute to make expenditures for the activities. The money used for creating all these infrastructures, is called "Capital Fund". Being 1st activity, the Schedule number assigned to the Capital Fund is Schedule-1.

- Sometimes, Reserve Fund is also created to handle the emergency situations. It is also like Capital Fund created by the Businessman or the Institution, hence it is Schedule-2.
- After opening of the Business or Institution, the Business or activities of the Institutions starts to work. The expenditure is started to be incurred to run the business and Income is also started to come. If the Income of the particular year is more than the Expenditure, it is profit and this amount of profit increases the Capital Fund; if Expenditure is more than the Income, it is loss to the business and Capital Fund is reduced by the amount of loss. This process goes on till the business is there.
- The expenditures are classified in different heads based on the nature of the expenditures and shown through different Schedules of Expenditure.

- Like wise expenditure, Income is also classified in different heads based on the nature of Income and shown in different Schedules.
- Sometimes, during the business the Advances/Loans are also taken which are termed as Liability and sometimes advances are also given to the employees or private parties which are current assets having effect on the Balance Sheet of the Business or the Institute.
- Receipts of money and Payments made of Revenue nature pertaining to a particular financial year become the part of Income and Expenditure of that year.
- The Schedules have been shown through the symbol of Buildings . The numbers of Schedules of Income and Expenditure may vary from Institute to Institute and

Business to Business. These may be more than as shown in this Book or may be Less, based on the nature of business and Institution.

- The readers may add or reduce the Schedules of Income or Expenditure or Assets and Liabilities as per their requirements keeping in view the activities of their business or their Institute.

Special thanks to

1. Sh. Rohit Singh
2. Sh R.K. Sonania
3. Mrs. Promila Indora

Author Signature

THANK YOU

9 798890 660725

Printed by Libri Plureos GmbH in Hamburg,
Germany